Cabaletta

Poems of a New York City Taxi Driver

by

Davidson Garrett

Finishing Line Press
Georgetown, Kentucky

Cabaletta

Poems of a New York City Taxi Driver

Copyright © 2022 by Davidson Garrett
ISBN 978-1-64662-727-1 First Edition
All rights reserved under International and Pan-American Copyright Conventions. No part of this book may be reproduced in any manner whatsoever without written permission from the publisher, except in the case of brief quotations embodied in critical articles and reviews.

ACKNOWLEDGMENTS

The following poems were published in earlier versions in the following magazines, anthologies, & literary journals:

The Stillwater Review (Sussex Community College), "Rush Hour"
From Somewhere to Nowhere: The End of the American Dream (Autonomedia), "A Taxi Driver's Götterdämmerung"
Saturday I Spent at Coney Island: Chapbook (Parachute Literary Arts), "Leaves of Gas: A Homage to Walt Whitman"
Meta-Land: Poets of the Palisades, Volume 2 (Poet's Press), "Driving Past 1040 Fifth Avenue"
Pears, Prose, and Poetry: (Poets Wear Prada/Eggplant Press), "A Hack's Elusive Love or Arthur Miller Lives"
Podium (the online literary journal of 92nd Street Y), "Villanelle"
Sensations Magazine Supplement #11, "Appalachian Spring in My Back Seat"
The Rainbow Project (Poets Wear Prada), "You Talking to Me?"

Publisher: Leah Huete de Maines
Editor: Christen Kincaid
Cover Photo: Lerone Pieters (Unsplash)
Author Photo: Roger Anderson
Cover Art & Design: Roger Anderson

Order online: www.finishinglinepress.com
also available on amazon.com

Author inquiries and mail orders:
Finishing Line Press
PO Box 1626
Georgetown, Kentucky 40324
USA

Table of Contents

Rush Hour 1

A Taxi Driver's Götterdämmerung 2

You Talking to Me? 4

Leaves of Gas: A Homage to Walt Whitman 6

Musing on the Fifteenth Anniversary of 9/11 8

Taxi TV 12

After Hurricane Sandy's Wrath 13

Driving Past 1040 Fifth Avenue 15

A Hack's Elusive Love or Arthur Miller Lives 17

Villanelle 19

Appalachian Spring in My Back Seat 20

Advice to a Beginning Driver 21

Chauffeuring the One Percent 24

Cabaletta 27

Rush Hour

Maybe Bartók?

It's all in the syncopation anyway,
a practiced pace to the subway

without breaking rhythm. I stop—
view toiletries in the drugstore window,

yet I misplaced my debit card
& must continue, shuddering from the thought

of imminent onslaught. A pear pleads
from a fruit vendor's stand. On approaching,

I witness weathered rot on green skin. Onward—
larghetto to underground stairs. Last stare

at the world above. A descent from one
atonal hell into another

as muted light collides
with cacophonous chaos.

Maybe Bartók,
definitely—Heavy Metal.

A Taxi Driver's Götterdämmerung
September 11, 2001

My downtown passenger, a banker from Barcelona—
we spoke of my love for the soprano Montserrat Caballé
that pristine day, driving this—Señor Financier
to the brass portals of American Express,

temple of commerce on Hudson's shore.
Early in the morning, I yawned tired air,
he paid the meter's fare and said—"Adios."
Zooming across the Westside Highway

in my *Yellow Zephyr*—
time for tourists at the Marriott Trade Center Hotel,
renovated midget adjacent to the looming twin giants.
Respite in the hack stand, I waited for an anxious hand

to hail my trusty Chevrolet
and whisk me away to another part of the island—
hopefully filling my poor palms with crisp bills.
Feeling a whiff of the almost autumn breeze,

my bald crown hugged the headrest,
lids lightly closed for a needed snooze.
Without warning, an earth-shattering—BOOM—
sounding like a million tympani

magnifying into decibels of Wagnerian proportion.
At first I thought it was a bomb—like the assault of '93,
leaping from the cab, heart drumming—
eyes glanced toward heaven.

Elastic flames like a snake's tongue
lanced through North Tower's steel skin
as a new epoch of terror fermented in fire.
Beams ripped amid primal screams—

sparkling glass rained down on my head
like waterfalls made of crystal confetti—
fumes of sulfurous clouds sparked fear;
the world shifted, seared in a crimson blaze of hate.

Like a mortal fleeing an incinerating dragon,
I escaped into my idling car—dented by debris—
explosions cracked like operatic thunder
while frantically clutching the steering wheel

for blessed life, afraid of what might come—
numb and dumbfounded in my own Immolation Scene.
A frightened foot pushed pedal to gas—
the auto dashed like a frenzied Valkyrie

toward Midtown—amid nervous skyscrapers.
In the rearview mirror, Valhalla
of the gods of gold and power
burned behind. No lyrical Rhinemaidens

or Brünnhilde's heroic high C
soaring over symphonic orchestra,
only my sea of briny tears—pianissimo,
accompanied by sirens.

You Talking to Me?

> *she flees from those who talk a lot about her...*
> —Alicia Partnoy

Nocturnal Manhattan, deprived of starlight.
I'm a zombie in the cab's front seat
numb with fatigue, birling my tired tires

on Lexington like a brain-fried automaton.
A frumpy, humped-back woman hails me—
stopping on a dime—an inch from her

orthopedic shoes; she stuffs her wide ass
in the back seat of my Crown Victoria
bellowing: "Port Authority!" We cruise

west on East 39th, rumbling to the beleaguered
bus station. Out of boredom, I pipe up:
"Do you live in Jersey?" Like a snarling

witch, she shrieks: "It's none of your business!"
Offended by her snotty insouciance,
I retort: "Got lots of friends down in Camden—

thought we might travel in the same circles?"
At that she snaps: "STOP THE CHAT AND DRIVE!"
I think to myself: Am I just a mere robot?

Is there a law against a cabbie
shooting the breeze with a passenger?
In the darkness of sinister midnight,

I deliver this grumpy [rhymes with itch]
to her hellish destination. She swipes
her credit card—slams the door with fury

as I take a verbal swipe at her.
Rolling down my side window, I shout:
"Lady, you deserve the Port Authority!"

Leaves of Gas: A Homage to Walt Whitman

> *I am with you, you men and women of a generation,*
> *or ever so many*
> *generations hence…*
> —Walt Whitman

Dearest Walt—you ferried to Manhattan with thousands of others
from the docks of Brooklyn, a different world in the 19th Century,
a world of industrial revolution—defining America as a robust

burgeoning country, a country inviting all tenacious people
to glean opportunities and build a great nation on this precious earth.
Here I am in the 21st Century, crossing with unabashed love

the same East River—driving over a fabled bridge in my taxi,
my humble little business on wheels, enabling me to subsidize
my poetic vocation in what morphed into a five borough city—

an ever-changing mega city since your very determined feet
trod its cobblestone streets. Viewing the skyline in afternoon
sun, I'm in awe of the architectural jewels—alluring glass towers

rising up to the bluest heavens. Deep inside myself, I know I'm only
a little speck in this vast plot of commerce, but a speck that shines
its own light—becoming a beating pulse of a whirling metropolis;

a metropolis with its crooked side streets, its bustling neighborhoods
brimming with trucks, cars, cabs and bikes, overflowing with
sidewalks of pedestrians, diverse denizens—all striving to explore

unlimited possibilities in the hubbub of an urban wonderland.
There is a tranquility within me, within my rhapsodic soul,
breathing hope—bound for the concrete island of infinite dreams.

As I begin my twelve-hour shift, my mind is at peace, filled with blessed contentment, solidifying a sense of purpose to my life while seeking to capture your romantic Whitmanesque promises.

My entire being rejoices in the power of the moment, finding answers to all transcendental questions, elated with the universe, until it all evaporates—when the first Jersey driver cuts me off.

Musing on the Fifteenth Anniversary of 9/11

With reflective anguish—
I can vividly smell
the devilish incense

of putrid smoke
drifting nightly
through my Midtown

apartment windows;
the acrid scent
of death

irritating
my nostrils
many weeks

after the surprise attack.
For hundreds of days
I drove by Ground Zero

like a creeping
lemon-colored caterpillar,
glancing somberly

at colossal cranes
& big ass bulldozers
tying up traffic

on the West Side Highway.
This war zone
appeared to be

a set of giant Tinkertoys
as time marched on
& tons of iron scaffolding

grew—floor by floor—
till finally
the one sleek tower

of Babel—
the redesigned
World Trade Center

rose to reach
the cerulean sky.
Except—this single

steel structure
was an only child
without an identical twin.

Horrific images
still swirl
in my mind,

even as fourteen years
have slipped away
& I clearly recall

the falling debris
denting my cab's hood
while waiting for fares

in the hotel hack stand
adjacent to the
unsuspecting

North Tower.
Shards of hard glass
spewed ferociously

from shattered windows
after the first plane
struck with vengeance—

raining showers of hate
& triggering
my fearful screams.

Images forever etched
in my brain's photo gallery
of an unlucky business woman

doused in jet fuel,
engulfed in fire,
rolling on the sidewalk—

as frantic citizens
desperately tried
to extinguish

her burned body.
I will be forever
haunted—

witnessing
commercial aircraft
looming low

over glittering Manhattan—
remembering
how my naked eyes

saw the shocking sight
of the second metal bird
strike the South Tower

in an explosion
of wicked flames
shaking the pavement

like a California earthquake
on that clear brisk morning.
I was a grateful cabbie

fortunate to flee
north toward Riverdale
with an English teacher

from Stuyvesant High,
a terrified backseat passenger.
We spoke soberly

how the world
would never be the same—
& we were right.

Taxi TV

annoying little TV screens
        TV screens on the back of
front seats in New York taxis
        white noise amid traffic jams
outdated weather reports
        with Al Roker jabbering
jabbering Al Roker jabbering
        outdated weather reports
cab rides offer no more quiet
        amid traffic jams no more quiet
movie reviews screaming nonsense
        on back of front seats
in New York taxis
        advertisements for pricey cafés
pricey pricey upscale cafés
        flashing out of bastard screens
the Off button won't shut off
        cab driver has no control
no control cab driver
        jabbering Al Roker
out of bastard screens
        a nonstop continuous loop
a continuous loop a continuous loop
        a continuous loop…loopy loopy loopy

After Hurricane Sandy's Wrath
November 2, 2012

Before dawn's first naked streak,
I spin wheels in the Financial District,
a corporate neighborhood—powerless,
moonless, blocks & blocks of pitch-blackness.
Barely seeing my hands before me,
my hissing motor invades the silence
as high beams of the intrepid cab
guide me through this surrealistic
maze, sadistically humbled by Mother Nature.
South Street Seaport destroyed, flooded
by a river's angry surge. Skyscrapers
appear like charcoal etchings—lifeless
in the hour when werewolves roam.
Subways sleep. Slowpoke buses nonexistent.
A few brave stick figures
stumble on invisible curbs
cautiously traversing crosswalks
bereft of working traffic signals.
This high-horsed town brought down
to its knees—the endless electricity
of dazzling Gotham burned out
from a flaming explosion,
mangling Con Ed's eastern substation.
In somber reverie, I muse how quickly
our lives suddenly shift—swift
as waves of water sinking islands.
A hipster on a bike with flashing beacons
becomes my compass, heading me south
on Broadway alongside Zuccotti Park—
unoccupied, except for a few defiant pigeons.

I'm always aware devils can strike—
while opening my owl eyes wider
for thieves who might rob me
on not-so-busy Beaver Street.
Car doors locked, auto crawls at a snail's pace—
desperately seeking souls
begging for a needed lift
out of this science fiction horror
created from a storm's wicked fury.
Who knew it would take a hurricane
for this persnickety old man
to be thrilled—for a fare to Brooklyn—
where there is still remnants of civilization
from flickering streetlamps
on Flatbush Avenue—
until—arriving at the devastated
carnival of Coney Island, & not far beyond—
the annihilated Rockaway Peninsula.

Driving Past 1040 Fifth Avenue

You were my childhood, Jacqueline Kennedy Onassis.
Such a rarified First Lady, glamming-up television news,
an inspiration to a gay boy harboring fanciful aspirations—
stuck in the hinterland of Louisiana. How I still remember

images of you at The Funeral; that long black veil
covering your grief-stricken face. Even at my young age,
I silently mourned as you orchestrated
your grave loss through dignified ritual.

Here in The Rotting Apple, my destiny reduced me
to a hack's life, struggling in my own tragedy
of unfulfilled dreams. For years, my cab whizzed
by the elegant edifice of your apartment house

gracing the corner of East Eighty-fifth and Fifth.
Oodles of times, I prayed your uniformed doorman
might flag me down—and BINGO: your celebrated self
glitzes up my back seat. And then, out of my adoring lips,

admiration and praise would trippingly roll off my tongue.
For your sake, you were spared. What a ritzy vicinity
you inhabited in your editorial days. But quite fitting
for Jackie O. Just a block from the cream-colored

Metropolitan Museum of Art, across the street
from Manhattan's emerald oasis, Central Park—
where you jogged around the sky-lined reservoir
appropriately renamed in your honor. Weeks before

your death, as I was trapped in southbound traffic
passing your palatial pad, I peered westward, saw you
resting on a park bench shaded by trees. Stoically beside
you, your companion, Mister Templesman, guarded you

from the ogling likes of me. Overblown sunglasses
hid your forlorn eyes, but I knew it was definitely you.
You appeared tranquil, at peace in the warm rays
of afternoon sun. My brain's black & white camera

captured this snapshot for my own eternity.
I should have double-parked to say hello—
however, legally I couldn't stop my vehicle
in a busy bus lane. Sorry I didn't risk a ticket now.

These days I buzz by your former dwelling,
recalling you with wistful affection. At times
I picture you as a diaphanous ghost
waving an arm for a taxi. Of course

your apparition is always adorned
in a smart Lilly Pulitzer day dress.
For me, an era of our town gone forever—
except in my memory's scrapbook.

A Hack's Elusive Love
or Arthur Miller Lives

Surprisingly, in my universe of taxi driving,
intersecting with New York's spaced-out humanity—
I'm still intrigued by otherworldly characters

I encounter behind my head. Met a fish food salesman
from Secaucus, hauled him in early evening twilight
during rush hour's syncopated prelude—

when whimsy surrenders to horn-honking & road rage.
My passenger—requested a ride to The Big Dinghy,
an upscale bar located somewhere near Water Street.

Navigating my cantankerous cab on a schizophrenic avenue
between farting buses & Subarus, I peered at Mister Jersey
from my rearview mirror. Aquamarine eyes & a crooked smile

embellished an adorable cartoon face
projecting a distinct sense of self. Out of pure boredom
or my usual free floating anxiety, I decided to probe

his Garden State brain, this fish food salesman
salivating for high-priced cocktails. Inquiring
about the pros & cons of a fishy profession—

selling morsels to sustain creatures of the aquarium—
the man simply stated, "It can be a lonely job"—
inspiring him to ramble about lucrative sales territory

up & down Atlantic's eastern shore. "I hawk
pet stores in Delaware one day, Philly the next."
Listening with my right ear—while challenging

a truck changing lanes, I mused to myself—
a loneliness, all for the sake of little flakes
thrown into glass prisons of tropical blues & gold—

simple sustenance for fresh water swimmers
trapped among wavering weeds & pebbles.
"Do you have a wife?"—I selfishly spouted out—

anxious perhaps to hook a future companion.
"She puts up with the traveling aspect of my life."
Disappointed, I pondered my own traveling aspect.

A competitive race, always seeking customers
for my back seat, even loud-mouthed shrimps
shouting addresses with patronizing contempt.

At our destination, depositing Willie Loman-of-the-Sea
before a bustling watering hole
frequented by bankers & loose women—

he paid me through the partition window
tossing over a handsome tip
& his personal business card

decorated with smiling mermaids. My worn eyes
made instant love as the lost catch faded into the night.
I dove back into my ocean of redundancy, fishing for fares.

Villanelle

Driving them, driving you, driving no one,
Clutching a steering wheel, lost in my cab—
What's the matter Ma'am? Isn't madness fun!

Hack license hangs on plastic partition—
Mug shot looks like a crackhead—ripe for rehab—
Driving them, driving you, driving no one.

Road rage: I morph into Attila the Hun—
When calm prevails: I'm flighty as Queen Mab—
What's the matter Ma'am? Isn't madness fun!

Men in drag hail me, shout: "Step-on-it-Hon!"
We buzz downtown, engrossed in FABULOUS gab—
Driving them, driving you, driving no one.

Head lights, tail lights, orange lights: Try not to run
Red lights, hauling a fussy East Side crab—
What's the matter Ma'am? Isn't madness fun!

Midnight mischief, a sly thief points lethal gun—
Grabs my cash! Guess who'll pay the meter's tab?
Driving them, driving you, driving no one—
What's the matter Ma'am? Isn't madness fun!

Appalachian Spring in My Back Seat

One of my shortest fares,
I only drove her
a block and a half

from a red apartment
building—to her school
on East 63rd Street.

But—as I peered
dumbstruck into
the cab's rearview mirror

witnessing the face
of Martha Graham, I knew
I was driving an iconic deity,

the mother of modern dance.

Advice to a Beginning Driver

So you want to be a taxi driver
in New York City? The first
question you must contemplate:

Do I have the temperament for the job?

And, my friend, what pray tell
am I suggesting by temperament?
Are you a confident driver? Do you

fully adhere to rules of safety
& speed limits? Is your body fit
to sustain twelve-hour shifts?

The Yes answers to these
three simple queries
are obvious, matter-of-fact

prerequisites for a nascent hack.
But by temperament—
I mean is your inner soul

prepared for the mind's
ever-present regrets
that the brain kaleidoscopes

conjuring long lost hopes
behind the steering wheel? Can
you embrace absurd humanity

staring at your hatted head
from behind the Plexiglass partition—
eventually berating or tormenting

or ignoring your very existence
while the rocketing auto
gusts like a metallic wind—

hauling these narcissistic denizens
around the five borough labyrinth?
Is there a natural Zen

within your deepest self
mellowing you to endure
flat tires, overheated engines

and harsh confrontations
by bullying traffic cops
writing out quota tickets

you will inevitably receive
because of reliable bad luck?
Are you able to stay serene

when greedy cabbies
race across five lanes
to guiltlessly steal

already acknowledged fares?
When passengers patronize,
will you strive to retort

with wry Damon Runyonisms
instead of snarky snideness?
Finally: Is your skin thick

as a rhinoceros
to demonstrate professionalism
for even the nastiest pimp

who flags you down
and treats you like a cheap whore?

Yes, dear youthful one,

being a courteous motorist
is an important component
for longevity

in this zany-but-never-boring
line of work. However,
the key word to consider—

and what ultimately decides
if you remain on the road:
TEMPERAMENT!

Chauffeuring the One Percent

As my lemon-colored vehicle
halted at a red light, a fist banged

on my right rear door.
Rotating my head

around, I was baffled
to see Mitt Romney

seeking my cab
on busy 2nd Avenue,

requesting to be taken
to La Guardia Airport.

Who would believe
the 2012 Republican

presidential nominee
would deign to ride

in my clunky Crown Vic?
This loser to Barack Obama

sported a backpack
over his broad shoulders

as he jumped into
my well-worn back seat.

Still surprised—carefully studying
his Ken-doll face

in the rearview mirror,
I wondered what-the-hell

to bullshit about
as the wheezing car's

balding tires
faithfully spun over

the Ed Koch Bridge
into Queens. Yes—

I could remain silent—
but this was too good

to be true. Stay away
from politics

I counseled myself
since I detested—Mitt's.

Finally, my jumbled
left wing brain

found common ground.
"You know Mr. Romney,

I always listened to
The Mormon Tabernacle Choir

on Sunday night radio
growing up in Louisiana."

He grinned gracefully
revealing his Chiclet teeth

& I was glad to have successfully
created some good will

after dumping him
at the dumpy Marine Air Terminal.

Such irony of Shakespearian
proportion, witnessing

this once would-be king
slowly processing past curbside check-in

without any paparazzi
flashing cameras, as he meekly settled

for the Delta Shuttle
instead of Air Force One.

Cabaletta

Steering my yellow canary
through discordant traffic
without a fare, the dashboard radio

blares vintage Joan Sutherland
negotiating coloratura passages
from Bellini's opera *I Puritani*.

Wistfully, I lament my repetitive
roulades—up & down concrete
streets—scouting for passengers.

Angelic tones of silver
pour through the airwaves:
the libretto's half-crazed Elvira

(anguished over lost love)
embellishes her plight
with the most brilliant trill

in modern musical history.
O to vocalize like the Australian diva,
I wouldn't be slaving in a taxi—

but receiving critical raves at La Scala.
Instead, I transport human cargo
on the isle of Manhattan, driving

a fender-dented sedan
with no orchestral accompaniment
to keep my tempo flowing.

The only aria I sing—
a sweet air of relief
following my shift's

horn-honking finale.
I then warble a joyful cabaletta—
another hack's opera bringing down its curtain.

Additional Acknowledgments

Thanks to Mark Nowak and members of the PEN Worker Writers School where several of these poems were born.

Many thanks to my friends and family who have given me encouragement and support for my artistic pursuits, especially Roger Anderson, Joseph Wisniewski, William Traylor, William Toner, Nafty Cohen, Dan Evans, Lulu LoLo, Taylor Caffery, Mary Ann Caffery, David Messineo, John J. Trause, Joel Allegretti, Warren Platt, John McDonagh, Louis Spirito, Eugenie Spirito, Seth Goldman, Amy Barone, Joseph Molloy, Laura Bair, and Dean Kostos.

Always appreciative to Molly Peacock for her poetic guidance over the years.

Grateful to Leah Huete de Maines, Christen Kincaid, and all of the staff at Finishing Line Press for making this chapbook a reality.

Davidson Garrett is a native of Louisiana and lives in New York City. He trained for the theatre at The American Academy of Dramatic Arts and is a graduate of The City College of New York. A longtime member of Actors' Equity and SAG/AFTRA, he worked in television, film and theatre for many years. His poetry has been published in *The New York Times, The Episcopal New Yorker, The Stillwater Review, Xavier Review from New Orleans, The Ekphrastic Review, First Literary Review East, 2 Bridges Review, Sensations Magazine, Impossible Archetype, Big City Lit*—and *Podium*, the literary journal of 92nd Street Y. Davidson is the author of two poetry collections: *King Lear of the Taxi*, published by Advent Purple Press and, most recently in 2020, *Arias of a Rhapsodic Spirit*, published by Kelsay Books. He has published three chapbooks: *To Tell the Truth I Wanted to be Kitty Carlisle and Other Poems*, published by Finishing Line Press; *Southern Low Protestant Departure: A Funeral Poem; and What Happened to the Man Who Taught Me Beowulf*, published by Advent Purple Press. In 2014, he was the 1st Place winner in the Juanita Torrence-Thompson International Poetry Competition, sponsored by Amulet Poetry Magazine. Davidson was the subject of the short film, *Davidson Garrett: Taxi Cab Poet* (by filmmaker Zardon Richardson) that was screened at the Jerome L. Greene Performance Space of WNYC Radio as part of the PEN World Voices Festival in 2019. He has been a member of the PEN Worker Writers School for several years. A Pushcart nominee, Davidson is a retired New York City Taxi Driver who drove a yellow cab off and on for forty years to subsidize his artistic pursuits.

www.ingramcontent.com/pod-product-compliance
Lightning Source LLC
LaVergne TN
LVHW041511070426
835507LV00012B/1479